FORGOTTEN YOUTH

Foster Youth

Leanne Currie-McGhee

ReferencePoint Press®

San Diego, CA

© 2017 ReferencePoint Press, Inc.
Printed in the United States

For more information, contact:
ReferencePoint Press, Inc.
PO Box 27779
San Diego, CA 92198
www.ReferencePointPress.com

LIBRARY OF CONGRESS CATALOGING-IN-PUBLICATION DATA

Names: Currie-McGhee, Leanne, author.
Title: Foster youth / by Leanne Currie-McGhee.
Description: San Diego, CA : ReferencePoint Press, Inc., [2017] | Series: Forgotten youth | Includes bibliographical references and index.
Identifiers: LCCN 2015046500 (print) | LCCN 2016001163 (ebook) | ISBN 9781601529763 (hardback) | ISBN 9781601529770 (epub)
Subjects: LCSH: Foster children--Juvenile literature. | Foster home care--Juvenile literature. | Child welfare--Juvenile literature.
Classification: LCC HV873 .C87 2017 (print) | LCC HV873 (ebook) | DDC 362.73/3083--dc23
LC record available at http://lccn.loc.gov/2015046500

Contents

Introduction

Traumatic Beginnings

As a child, Crystal Bentley did all of the things that other kids do: she went to school, she played with friends, she did her chores. But Crystal Bentley was not like other kids. Bentley was a foster youth—a ward of the state. She was placed in foster care at the age of two because her mother, a drug addict, paid more attention to her own needs than to the needs of her daughter. Endangered by neglect, Bentley was removed from her home; she spent sixteen years in foster care. During that time, she shifted between foster homes, her mother's home, and group homes (which provide residential care for several foster children who are supervised by staff known as group mothers and group fathers). Her foster care experience included one set of foster parents who verbally abused her and a foster brother who molested her. Eventually, at age eighteen, Bentley aged out of the system—meaning she reached the age when foster care and all associated services end. From that point forward, Bentley was on her own. The system that was meant to provide safety and stability had largely failed Bentley.

Not all foster care stories are so traumatic. For some youngsters, foster care provides the lifesaving support they desperately need. This is what happened to Isaiah, who was born with congenital myotonic dystrophy—a muscle-wasting disease that put him in a wheelchair and required him to use a feeding tube. His condition made good-quality care even more imperative. But Isaiah's mother, with whom he lived, did not provide this care. Severe medical neglect forced social workers to remove Isaiah from his home. He was placed in a foster care treatment center for medically fragile children so that he could obtain the specialized care he needed. During this period, Isaiah's father decided to seek custody of his son. Toward that end, he began working with social workers and treatment facility staff to gain the needed skills and knowledge to care for Isaiah. He visited often and worked closely with the staff to learn how to feed Isaiah through a feeding tube and take care of his other medical and emotional needs. After twenty-one months, father and son were reunited, and Isaiah's father received full custody—enabling the two to form new bonds of trust and love.

The stories of Isaiah and Crystal illustrate the triumphs and failings of foster care. Nearly half a million US youths enter the foster care system each year because they are abused or neglected by their parents. Some youngsters thrive, but others founder. Whichever the outcome, their pain, their struggles, and their stories are largely hidden from public view. Most people do not hear about the workings of the foster care system until a tragedy occurs. Even then, it is sometimes hard to understand the system, its methods, and its purpose.

Surviving a System

Young people who have been in foster care describe an array of complex and sometimes conflicting feelings about themselves, their parents, their foster families, and the foster care system. It is not surprising that foster youth have such a mix of feelings. The idea of being mistreated by one's parents is bad enough, but these youths continue to face hardships. They are pulled from the only homes they know, moved into homes with strangers, and transferred into schools they have never seen before, with kids they have never met—always with the hope that they can somehow pick up where they left off. And always in the background is the knowledge that they could one day be returned to their parents—but without any guarantees of something better than they left. Just one of these actions would cause most people grief. But foster kids must deal with all of them—and sometimes all at once.

The primary goal of foster care is to eventually place youngsters in permanent homes—either returning them to their own homes or adopting them into others. To accomplish that goal, foster care systems all across the country often must remove

5

Some children end up being adopted by their foster parents. Here, a happy mother poses with her adopted daughters.

young people from their homes and temporarily place them in other settings. These other settings include foster families, group homes, or other facilities whose purpose is to provide a safe and stable environment that meets the physical, emotional, and medical needs of the young people in their care.

Despite the best efforts of those who work in these systems, foster care in America has many flaws. The quality of foster care providers is far from consistent. Siblings are often separated from each other, and efforts to reunite parents and children often fail after many stops and starts. Likewise, caseworkers experience huge and sometimes impossible caseloads. Often these problems result in young people being shuttled from one foster family to another, with little hope of achieving a permanent home. This was Matthew Nelson's experience. By age fifteen he had lived in sixteen different foster homes. He always kept a bag packed, ready for his next move, never feeling that he had a place to call home. His Department of Children and Family Services records fill up two large folders—and yet the records of his years in foster care are incomplete. Essentially, it seems like he was forgotten. "Bleak. There's just no other word for it," Lee Nelson, foster father to Matthew, says of Matthew's experience in the system. "It's a story of misjudgments and misplacements and people giving up."[1] For Matthew, there was a happy ending. After experiencing such chaos, he was adopted by Nelson. He had beaten the odds.

Lasting Impact

Matthew's experience of being adopted after so many years in foster care is not typical. According to the North American Council on Adoptable Children, the average age of children who are adopted from foster care is about seven years old. The longer a young person remains in foster care, the less likely he or she will be adopted by a family. Lisa Basile grew up in the foster care system—and remained there until she reached adulthood. Basile's parents were both drug users who were unable to care for her, which is why she was placed in foster care. She lived with the same foster family until her eighteenth birthday, at which time she was considered by the state to be an adult. Her foster care experience was as positive as foster care can be. Her foster family gave her love and support in all areas of her life. But even a loving foster family cannot completely erase the feelings of inadequacy that many foster youth carry around with them—even long after they have left foster

> "Bleak. There's just no other word for it."[1]
>
> —Lee Nelson, a foster father on his adopted son's foster care experience.

care. Basile eventually went on to college and is now a successful writer and editor. Yet she explains that the effects of growing up in foster care never go away. "It is even harder to shake off that stigma—that feeling that I'm sort of always floating, anchor-less," writes Basile. "Despite my 'new' life, I deal with feelings of worth-lessness and loss daily; it's a sort of lasting PTSD [post-traumatic stress disorder] that hovers like a rain cloud."[2]

Chapter 1

The Foster Care System

Every year in the United States, thousands of young people are removed from their homes and placed in foster care. In 2014, according to the most recent statistics from the federal Adoption and Foster Care Analysis and Reporting System (AFCARS), 415,219 children and teens were living in foster care. The goal of foster care is to provide these youngsters a temporary but stable and consistent home life. While they are in foster care, their parents work with the local department of children's services (DCS) to create a safe and stable home for them. In the event that they cannot be returned to their parents, the goal is then to provide the children and teens with a stable, permanent home through adoption as soon as possible.

Most young people who enter foster care do so because their parents or legal guardians do not provide proper care. According to the National Child Abuse and Neglect Data System, neglect is the single biggest cause of foster care placements. Nearly 80 percent of youths in foster care were neglected, and most of these cases stem from parental drug abuse. Studies by the Child Welfare League of America reveal that substance abuse is a factor in at least 75 percent of all foster care placements. "Young children are coming into state custody in unprecedented numbers. This is primarily being driven by parental heroin use,"[3] writes Cindy Walcott, Vermont's deputy commissioner for family services.

Anne Bissell is one of those parents whose heroin use stole her ability to care for her children. There were many times when she was strung out on heroin, lying on the bathroom floor, and ignoring their basic needs, including providing food, monitoring their hygiene, and making sure they went to school. She specifically recalls what she missed in connection with her son. When she was high, she says, "I wasn't there to make sure he wasn't getting hit by a car. I wasn't there to make sure he's brushing his teeth and helping him get dressed in the morning. I wasn't there for any of that stuff."[4]

How an Investigation Begins

Although foster care systems vary from state to state, the overall process is roughly the same throughout the country. Typically, foster care removal starts with a call to a county's DCS from anyone who suspects abuse or neglect. A call may be from a neighbor who observes young children being left alone at home without supervision or someone who observes a parent using drugs while their children are around. Many states advertise toll-free numbers for people to call if they suspect problems, and these states receive thousands of calls. In 2015, for instance, the Colorado Department of Human Services toll-free hotline received nearly 205,000 reports of suspected child abuse or neglect.

Other reports come from social workers, medical and mental health professionals, teachers, and child care providers—all of whom are required by law to report suspected abuse or neglect. For example, pediatricians are required to notify child welfare services if they suspect that young patients with frequent bruises and broken bones are being abused by parents or other caregivers.

In most states child welfare agencies have a process for screening calls and reports before deciding whether to act on them. Of the 205,000 calls to Colorado's state hotline in 2015, a total of 88,441 resulted in further investigation; of these, 32,709 triggered an assessment by the state's child welfare agency. All

> "I wasn't there to make sure he wasn't getting hit by a car. I wasn't there to make sure he's brushing his teeth and helping him get dressed in the morning. I wasn't there for any of that stuff."[4]
>
> —Anne Bissell, whose son went into foster care.

Foster Care Demographics

A 2015 federal report highlights key characteristics of youth who were in foster care the previous year. The statistics, gathered by the Adoption and Foster Care Analysis and Reporting System (AFCARS), show that in 2014: males outnumbered females in foster care; whites represented the largest percentage of youth in foster care; and the most common lengths of time spent in foster care fell between one and eleven months.

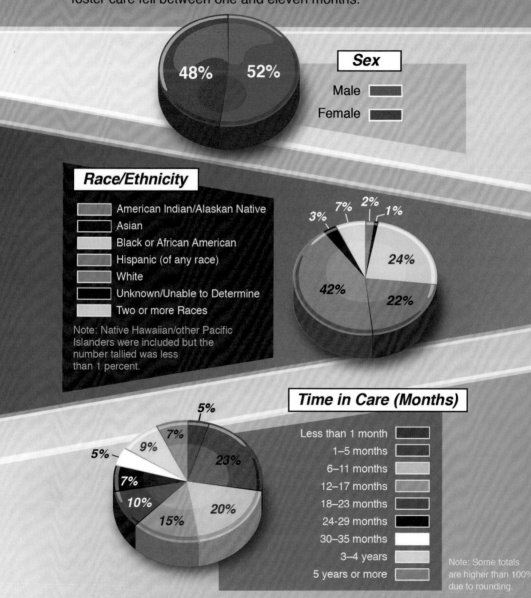

Sex

Male
Female

Race/Ethnicity

American Indian/Alaskan Native
Asian
Black or African American
Hispanic (of any race)
White
Unknown/Unable to Determine
Two or more Races

Note: Native Hawaiian/other Pacific Islanders were included but the number tallied was less than 1 percent.

3% 7% 2% 1%
24%
42% 22%

Time in Care (Months)

5%
7%
5% 9%
23%
7%
10% 20%
15%

Less than 1 month
1–5 months
6–11 months
12–17 months
18–23 months
24-29 months
30–35 months
3–4 years
5 years or more

Note: Some totals are higher than 100% due to rounding.

Source: US Department of Health and Human Services, "The AFCARS Report," July 2015. www.acf.hhs.gov.

states require the local DCS to initiate an investigation in a timely manner, generally within seventy-two hours, once they begin an assessment.

What Occurs During an Investigation

Once an investigation is initiated, DCS specialists talk to all involved in the situation. This could include parents, guardians, neighbors, and the young person who is the subject of concern. They may also speak with outside people, such as teachers or day care providers, to get a clearer picture of the situation. The DCS does not need parental permission to talk to alleged victims and their siblings, and often these interviews occur at school. A DCS specialist will also visit the family home to discuss the report and gather more information. Parents and all other individuals may refuse to be interviewed, but the investigation will still proceed. During an investigation, the youth may continue to reside with the family or, if an investigator believes that the youngster is in danger, he or she will be placed in temporary foster care. Within a few days a judge must determine whether the youth should stay in foster care or return home for the duration of the investigation.

The entire investigation is usually completed within thirty days. Even when neglect and abuse are not found, the assessment often identifies services that might assist the family. If, however, the assessment determines that abuse or neglect is taking place, the case is sent to family court for a decision regarding foster care or other services. The federal Administration for Children and Families 2014 report estimates that 3.6 million referrals were made to state child welfare agencies, involving 6.6 million children, for possible neglect or abuse. Of these, 702,000 were determined to be victims of abuse or neglect and were subject to action by the courts.

Cases such as these are normally heard in family courts, in which a single judge hears and makes decisions on cases that involve custody, divorce, and neglect or abuse. A family court judge will hear all DCS evidence and recommendations; often parents will speak, and sometimes the judge will also hear from the youngster. On the basis of the evidence, the judge will decide

11

whether the home is unsafe for the youth. If that is the judge's finding, the youth will be placed in foster care, or if he or she has already been placed in short-term care due to potential endangerment, the youth will remain in foster care. Typically, the youth is placed in temporary foster care that same day; from the moment of the ruling, he or she is a ward of the state.

Finding Foster Care Parents

Once the judge has determined that the young person should be removed from the home, the search begins for a long-term foster family. Although a caseworker may have determined some possibilities for long-term foster care during the investigation, he or she cannot set anything up until the judge makes a decision.

Relatives are often the first choice because research shows that youngsters fare better with people they know than with strangers. For example, only 6 percent of kids placed with relatives try to run away, compared with 16 percent in traditional foster homes and 35 percent in group homes, according to the Center for Law and Social Policy, an antipoverty advocacy agency in Washington, DC. In most states, relatives do not need to obtain a foster care license, but their homes must be assessed according to standards equivalent to those required for a license and approved by a county social worker. If they decide to become foster parents, a youth's relatives may be required to meet these requirements while the youth remains in temporary foster care.

If relatives are not able or willing to become foster parents, then social workers move on to find available foster parents within the system. These individuals have had their foster parent applications accepted and have received training by the agencies overseeing foster care. Most states have the same basic requirements for people who wish to become foster parents: They must be at least twenty-one years old, pass a background check, complete CPR training, and show that they have a house or apartment that meets standards. Foster parents receive monetary assistance for each child they foster, but the amount is just enough to cover the child's basic needs. States require that foster parents have

A grandmother holds her granddaughter. Authorities often try to place foster children with a relative, since youngsters tend to fare better when they live with someone they know.

sufficient income to support themselves without foster care assistance. Prospective foster parents must complete a preservice training to learn about parenting skills and special needs, such as dealing with the aftermath of abuse or sexual molestation that foster children may have experienced.

Voluntary Foster Care Placement

It is hard to imagine parents giving up their children voluntarily, but these cases occur when parents feel overwhelmed or incapable of providing care. Some parents choose this option because they have become homeless and want their children to live in a home while they work on their situation. Others choose this because they may have medical needs to attend to and cannot currently care for their children. Briana was eleven years old and living in North Carolina when her mother gave her up. Her family was poor, and two of her siblings also lived at home, along with a grandfather suffering from Alzheimer's disease. "My grandfather was bad, and my mom had to focus on him. She couldn't handle it all, so she brought us [to a foster care group home]." Briana chose to stay in the group home past age eighteen so that she could prepare for college and independent life. (North Carolina is one of the states that allows young people to remain in foster care until age twenty-one.)

Quoted in Beth Walton, "Finding a Home: Need for Foster Care Outpacing Resources," *Asheville (NC) Citizen-Times*, August 29, 2015. www.citizen-times.com.

Matching foster parents to a youth is typically overseen by a social worker within the DCS or by a private company hired by the state. "We keep looking till we find a good match," says Iona LaBaw, a foster parent specialist supervisor in Tippecanoe, Indiana. "Sometimes it can be one phone call, but sometimes it can take hours. . . . Some of it depends on the special needs of the children. We do have children with special needs, and the trauma that kids go through—even being removed from their biological home can be traumatic."[5] Social workers attempt to match a youth with a family that shares a similar background— for example, the same religious affiliation, similar ethnicity, close geographic proximity to the youth's family home, and a single- or two-parent family structure. Additionally, if the placement involves siblings, social workers attempt to keep the siblings together, but it is not always possible. For example, despite the best efforts of social workers in Tennessee, 25 percent of sibling groups in that state were separated in in 2015. Similarly, a New York City study showed that 22 percent of youths who entered foster care at the same time as their siblings were separated.

The Challenges of Placement

Once youngsters are placed in a home, foster parents are responsible for their daily care. That means they provide food and clothing, ensure the kids go to school, take them to doctor and dentist appointments, and take part in all of the other daily activities that parents engage in with their kids.

Foster parents have limitations, however. They are not legally responsible for the youths in their care and cannot make major decisions for them. For example, foster parents must comply with the court's decisions on how often and when the youths visit their parents. Foster parents also cannot move their young charges to another location, change their school, or make decisions about medical treatment without court permission. The power to make these decisions remains with the state until the youngsters are reunited with their parents, adopted, or become legal adults.

Although the goal of foster care is to provide a stable living situation, this does not always occur. Foster parents might decide they cannot continue to care for the youths who have been placed with them. Sometimes a youth and foster parents simply do not get along. Sometimes a youngster acts out or runs away, making an already difficult situation harder. Young people in foster care often carry a lot of anger, fear, and distrust. A foster parent's inability to deal with these emotions can further damage the relationship. The DCS tries to address these situations by providing training for foster parents and counseling for youths in foster care, but training and counseling do not always solve the problems.

When a foster care situation does not work out, the youth is then placed with another family or in a group home. The danger is that this becomes a cycle, particularly as the youth grows older.

Cris Beam is a foster mother and the author of the acclaimed book *To the End of June: The Intimate Life of American Foster Care*. She explains that young people often act out in response to the frightening experiences they have undergone and the trauma of being taken from their families. Their actions, in turn, can scare off ill-prepared foster parents, which then forces caseworkers to look for yet another family or facility to provide temporary care that may or may not last while the search for a permanent home continues.

Long-Term Goals

Once in foster care, the DCS aims to provide young people with a permanent home as quickly as possible. However, the wait for this can be long. In 2014, according to the latest AFCARS statistics, the average stay in foster care was 19.5 months. During this time youngsters are in a waiting mode—waiting to see whether they will return to their family or be adopted by another family.

Family reunification occurs in about half of the cases. In 2014, for instance, 51 percent of those who exited foster care were reunited with their parent(s). Janelle is one young woman who was successfully reunited with her mother, although it was not an easy road. Janelle's mother often felt angry and was unable to provide the day-to-day care her children needed, so she decided she wanted them to live with their aunt. Janelle's mother placed them in the foster care system, with the agreement that they would receive kinship care from their aunt. Janelle and her brother had to spend one month at a temporary foster home while their aunt was approved by the system, and then they were placed with their aunt, whom they stayed with for three years. During this time Janelle's mother received counsel-

> "My mother used to get so angry whenever someone would give her attitude. She would yell at the top of her lungs while cussing them out. But since we'd left, it seemed like she'd learned how to control that."[6]
>
> —Janelle, a foster youth.

16

The number of US youth in foster care rose by more than seventeen thousand between 2011 and 2014, according to a 2015 federal report. The rise is attributed to various factors, including increased drug use by parents and heightened state efforts in investigating reports of child neglect and abuse.

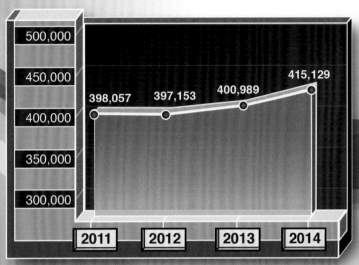

Source: US Department of Health and Human Services, "The AFCARS Report," July 2015. www.acf.hhs.gov.

ing, learned to deal with anger issues, and had supervised visits with her children. Eventually Janelle and her brother moved back in with their mother. Although it was not easy, through counseling and communicating Janelle and her mother reestablished a good relationship, and her mother provided a safe home. "She'd made many changes while my brother and I were gone," Janelle writes. "I think one of the biggest changes she made was with her anger. My mother used to get so angry whenever someone would give her attitude. She would yell at the top of her lungs while cussing them out. But since we'd left, it seemed like she'd learned how to control that. She seemed calmer, like she was at peace with herself."[6]

Reunification is not always possible. In other cases, parental rights are terminated when it becomes clear that the youth's parents

Overworked Caseworkers

Most caseworkers in foster care are dedicated to their jobs and want to give young people the best care possible. But many caseworkers have a heavy caseload. This means they have little time to give each youth's case any personal attention. Julia Wasvick, a child welfare worker in Mississippi, laments, "How could any caseworker with a caseload of 70 to 100 manage to go out and see the children? I mean, that's impossible." Janet Atkins, who has been working as a social worker for child welfare agencies in California since 1986, comments that caseloads are so high that social workers have to make hard choices—they either visit the families and children under their watch or do the paperwork that is required by law. In California, caseworkers have at least fifty-four cases at one time. "There's no way you can see 54 children once a month and still do the rest," says Atkins.

ABC News, "Foster Care System Stretched Too Far," 2014. http://abcnews.go.com.

are unable or unwilling to do what is required to provide a safe home. In this case, the child remains in foster care with the goal of adoption, which occurred for 21 percent of those who exited foster care in 2014. But as youngsters age, adoption becomes less likely. Those who are not adopted or reunited end up either aging out of the system or moving on to live permanently with another family member or guardian.

Around 10 percent of young people in foster care do not achieve a long-term goal of a permanent home. Instead, they are emancipated when they turn eighteen. Emancipation is when a youth becomes a legal adult while still in foster care. At this point, he or she is released from foster care to be independent—often with little or no support. Although financial and housing services are available to help them, many young adults are unaware of these programs and encounter difficulties as they try to find their own way in the world.

Lifetime Impact

Whatever their experiences in foster care, young people who have gone through the system tend to feel its impact for the rest of their lives. Festus Ohan is where he wants to be, but he will never forget the hardships he endured. Ohan came through his foster care experience as a strong young man, but it was a difficult road. He was abandoned by his father, then cycled through seven or eight foster homes before he aged out. During his time in foster care, Ohan says, his foster parents did not support his desire to attend college and medical school. He was essentially left to his own devices. Despite his difficult childhood, Ohan graduated from the University of California, Riverside, with a degree in neuroscience and has received acceptance letters from several medical schools throughout the country. Even while he was achieving success at school, Ohan remembers that there were still nights that he "went to bed in tears crying, praying, asking God 'why did this happen to me?'"[7]

> "I went to bed in tears crying, praying, asking God 'why did this happen to me?'"[7]
>
> —Festus Ohan, a former foster youth.

Even young adults like Ohan deal with the lasting effects of being taken from their families and placed in other care. How they deal with these situations is determined both by the support they receive and by their own inner strength.

Chapter 2

Removal

Lisa Basile clearly remembers the day the social workers came to take her and her brother to their new foster families. They had both been staying temporarily with their great-aunt until their caseworker could find them a foster family. But one family for the two of them could not be found, so they were sent to separate houses—and separate lives. Basile's new foster family was within walking distance of her great-aunt's house, and she walked to her new home on her own. "No one walked with me. I brought a few bags and a box. I said goodbye to my brother, who drove away in a car," Basile later recalled. "The loneliness had no end. That day, the social worker made the mistake of telling me that the family 'gave back' a younger girl once, leaving me to worry about homelessness for the next three years."[8]

Jamie Schwandt also clearly remembers the day the social workers came to take him from his drug-addicted parents to his new foster home. "I was a frightened eighth-grader when without explanation, I was loaded into a car and deposited on the door-step of my first foster family,"[9] he later recalled.

Finding Out

The experiences described by Basile and Schwandt are not uncommon. Although young people being placed in foster care have most likely been interviewed by social workers and may have even appeared in court before a judge, they often do not realize that they are being removed from their homes and placed with another family until it actually happens. Heather remembers her abrupt introduction to foster care: "I was seven when a case worker showed up and asked me if I wanted to go to McDonalds for something to eat, and my mom telling me that it was ok that she just wanted to talk to me. Little did I know that I was really being taken from my mom and put into foster care."[10]

Sometimes, seemingly out of the blue, a caseworker appears and announces that it is time to leave. This might be because it is deemed unsafe to leave youngsters in their homes while the courts determine what should take place. One girl and her siblings lived with an aunt, who was their guardian. The aunt, however, was abusing them. A woman from church, whom they were close to, called the DCS because she suspected this abuse, and DCS investigated. The children were interviewed, but because they were scared of what might happen, they lied and said the aunt did not abuse them. As months passed, the girl assumed that the investigation was over. And then one day a social worker showed up at school. "Alicia, Christopher and I were called out of class. When we got to the office our social worker was there, and said, 'You're coming with me,'" she recalls. "I was happy that we would finally be moving but I was crying because I didn't know where I was going to go. I had no idea why our social worker came that day, but looking back, my guess is that our church mom called the foster care system again."[11]

> "I was a frightened eighth-grader when without explanation, I was loaded into a car and deposited on the doorstep of my first foster family."[9]
>
> —Jamie Schwandt, a former foster youth.

No Time to Prepare

Typically, young people being placed in foster care have little time to prepare. Most have only enough time to quickly pack a bag of essentials. If the youth does not have a suitcase—and many do not—their only choice may be to use a common plastic trash bag. Katy Gibson entered foster care at age two but moved in and out of various homes throughout her childhood. When she packed her belongings, she recalls, her "suitcase" was a trash bag. "There is nothing more degrading and belittling than having to shove your belongings into a big black trash bag!" she writes. "As a foster care child, there is not a lot that is actually yours. . . . Shoving the things you love most, into something intended for trash, makes you feel lower than dirt."[12]

Once packed, it is time to say good-bye—to parents (or foster parents, if moving from one foster home to another), pets, siblings, or other family members who share the house. Quick good-byes become a familiar routine to many youngsters in foster care. Campbell, a former foster youth, describes the ritual she developed whenever she moved to a new foster home. "I would look around my room one last time," Campbell remembers. "Goodbye bed! Goodbye pillow. Goodbye pets! Goodbye toys. When I was younger I would hug my foster siblings goodbye. I loved them. I always loved them."[13] For Campbell and other foster youth, the good-byes are agony.

Separated Siblings

One of the hardest parts of being placed in foster care or leaving one foster home for another is being separated from siblings. Caseworkers try to keep siblings together, but often they cannot do so because available foster families are not always able or willing to take them. A foster family might have room for only one child, for instance, or the family might be willing to take a young child but not an older one. These separations can be devastating to youngsters because their last connection to family is torn away, and they must take the arduous journey through foster care on their own. For Briana, the separation from her sister is a sharp memory that does not fade. "I'll never forget when I entered my second placement in foster care. It was January 27, 2006, the day I was separated from my sister," Briana writes. "I was 15 at the time, and had only entered foster care a month before. My sister (who is nine years younger) was in the car with the social worker, the driver and myself. She was crying her eyes out as she hugged me goodbye."[14] Leaving behind an abusive mother, Briana and her sister were placed in the same home. But when the social worker returned a month later, Briana's sister was moved to their grandparent's house, and Briana was taken to a residential treatment center. This is a group home specifically for youth who are experiencing emotional issues and need more intense therapeutic services.

A teenage girl departs, carrying some of her belongings. Children who are taken from their homes often must leave quickly, sometimes bringing with them only what they can carry in a plastic bag.

In addition to experiencing the pain of parting from one another, youngsters fear that they will not see their siblings again. This fear is justified. Sometimes it is months or even years before they do see each other again due to being placed far apart. Arlene, age sixteen, remembers the pain of leaving her sister, and the worry that came after the separation. "When [they] moved us and placed us all in different homes I felt as if God was punishing me for something. It broke my heart. . . . I had sleepless nights wondering: Is my sister OK?"[15] she writes.

Mixed Emotions

Leaving siblings and everything else that is familiar makes the entry into foster care a frightening experience no matter how bad the situation is at home. The emotions that accompany leaving their families and starting on a new and unpredictable path are complex. Feelings of relief at leaving abusive or neglectful parents might be tempered by fear of the unknown. Anger is another common emotion—sometimes stemming from the failures of their parents and other times at the idea of having no say in their own lives. Many feel all of these emotions at once.

Yaya experienced a sense of freedom when she was taken from her mother. For years she had watched her mother endure brutal beatings by a man whom her mother would not leave. "At age 9, I entered a moment in my life that would change my future. I waved goodbye to the woman that gave birth to me," Yaya writes. "I was in a police car, on my way to foster care. At that moment, I felt liberated because I would no longer endure the pain of watching my mom suffer down a path of self-destruction."[16] Although Yaya did not know what lay ahead, she felt relief during her first moments of leaving.

> "I was in a police car, on my way to foster care. At that moment, I felt liberated because I would no longer endure the pain of watching my mom suffer down a path of self-destruction."[16]
>
> —Yaya, a former foster youth.

Sibling Summer Camp

One of the most wrenching aspects for foster youth is being separated from their brothers and sisters. Leaving home and their parents is hard enough, but being separated from siblings means they have to face the future alone. A major fear of many young people, when separated from siblings, is that they will lose touch with one another. Lynn Price, who grew up in foster care, is working to ensure this does not happen. Price founded Camp To Belong in Las Vegas in 1995. Today the camp has locations in seven US states and in Australia, and it has connected more than four thousand young people during the camp's week-long sessions.

At the camp, siblings separated by foster care reunite for a week of typical camp fun—a ropes course, swimming, a talent show, and family birthday celebrations since many of these siblings do not get to celebrate together. "You see tears, you see a lot of hugs," says Karen Schimmels, the director of Camp To Belong Oregon. "They're just really happy to be together."

Rheana Murray, "Summer Camp Reconnects Siblings Separated by Foster Care System," *Good Morning America*, August 21, 2014. https://gma.yahoo.com.

Michelle experienced an altogether different set of emotions when she realized she was going to foster care a second time. The first time that she was in foster care lasted only a few weeks before she was returned to her mother. A few months later, Michelle recalls, she was called to the school nurse's office to take a call from her mother. Her mother was upset and told Michelle to take her little sister and leave the school. Michelle started hyperventilating, and the school nurse told her to stay put. Soon after, Michelle was told that a social worker was coming to pick her up from school. "I was terrified," she remembers. "I just wanted to go home."[17] Michelle remained in foster care until she aged out.

For some young people, leaving a foster family is as traumatic as leaving their own parents. Foster families give up their young charges for various reasons: The foster family might be moving, or the foster parents might be unable to handle a youth's behavioral or medical issues. Dylan had lived with his foster family for five months and had become very close to his foster father. One night, his foster father took him on what seemed like a special weekend trip to Chicago. "At dinner, I felt the rug pull out from underneath me when he told me he had accepted a job in Washington, DC," Dylan remembers. "At first I was super excited. Then he said, 'I have to move and thought bringing you to Chicago might soften the blow.'" It was then that Dylan, who was fourteen at the time, realized he would not be going with the family to Washington, DC. "I couldn't contain my sadness. I started crying."[18] Dylan ultimately lived in twenty-three different homes during his years in foster care.

Many youngsters in foster care develop emotional barriers as a defense against so much pain, loss, and sadness. To ease the difficulty of leaving, for example, they simply stop allowing themselves to feel any attachment to the people around them. Debbie

A young boy stares out a window. Children in foster care often develop emotional barriers to protect themselves from the sadness of moving from home to home.

was removed from her home and separated from her sisters at age five. By age fifteen she had already lived in eleven or twelve foster homes. Debbie explains what usually happened when the caseworker showed up at her foster home: "I would get back from school, my bags were packed, I didn't have time to say goodbye to anyone." She says, "You have to build up a wall so you don't get close."[19] Like many young people in foster care, Debbie emotionally closed herself off from others as she dealt with the feelings of rejection and insecurity that accompany being constantly taken from people and places.

Nowhere to Go

Once taken from their homes, youngsters are rarely immediately taken to a new home. Instead, there is a wait—sometimes just hours and other times days—to find them a foster family. A caseworker may identify potential placements during an investigation, but he or she cannot set one up until an official court ruling determines that the youth is being placed in foster care. During short waiting periods, the youth is often brought to the social worker's office while he or she searches for a family.

Waiting in an office, after the pain of being taken from his or her family, adds to the youth's stress and worry. First, the social worker will try to identify a relative to take the youth. If kinship care is not available, the caseworker must find a foster family that is willing to take the youth. The caseworker searches through his or her available families and attempts to make a match. This can result in an often long, nervous wait in an office.

The wait can extend to overnight. Some departments have created makeshift homes for situations such as these. In Arizona, several youths have ended up sleeping inside one of the dozen or more DCS office buildings throughout Maricopa and Pima Counties. "We have tried to make do with what we have. We have volunteers that bring in and donate food. We have beds here. We have cribs. We have a washing machine and dryer. We have a shower. This is not the place to put a kid,"[20] DCS program manager Gene Burns explains. This instability leads to increased anxiety in an already stressful situation.

War Torn

Post-traumatic stress disorder (PTSD) is typically associated with veterans who have developed extreme anxieties after experiencing the trauma of war. Symptoms of PTSD include panic attacks, sleep issues, and reexperiencing the trauma through nightmares or flashbacks. A study by researchers at Harvard University and the University of Michigan reveals that foster youth are twice as likely as veterans to develop PTSD. That study, known as the Northwest Foster Care Alumni Study, followed 659 foster care alumni of the Oregon and Washington state welfare agencies. Researchers found one in four alumni had experienced PTSD in the previous twelve months, and more than half of them had experienced at least one mental health problem such as depression, social phobia, or panic syndrome. Factors identified as contributing to this disorder in former foster youth include the initial circumstances that led to foster care, frequent placements, instability, and a lack of permanent support.

What is worse is that some youngsters, even after waiting at a DCS office, will not end up with families. States all over the country are seeing a dearth of foster parents. As an example, the number of kids put into foster care by North Carolina's Division of Social Services has risen nearly 19 percent since 2012, from 8,599 then to 10,228 in 2015. At the same time, the number of families willing to foster a youth dropped by six hundred, with fewer than seven thousand licensed homes across the state. Many of these young people end up in group homes, an institutional setting where youths are housed together with live-in staff who serve as house parents.

The Next Step

Once a youth's placement is settled, then he or she moves on to a new home. No matter how welcoming the foster family is, the experience is strange and surreal to the youth. Although social workers attempt to place a youngster in an area close to his or her home, this does not always occur, so the youth may end up in an entirely unknown region and may have to attend a different school. Then the youth must walk into a house or an apartment to be introduced to a stranger who is meant to act as a temporary parent and meet all of the family in the home. In addition to all of the emotional baggage the young person is dealing with, now he or she has to acclimate to this totally new situation.

An anonymous former foster youth remembers the odd feeling of walking into a strange house after he and his brothers were removed from their home. "That first day in the home was extremely awkward. No matter how much someone opens his or her home to you the awkwardness is still there. We were going to a new home where we didn't know how they lived or how they did things. You don't know their routine, their rules or expectations," he writes. "They did eventually cover some of the rules and tried

A young girl waits alone. Foster children often must wait for hours or even overnight until a home can be found.

to make us feel as comfortable as possible given the situation. All we had were the clothes on our back and a few things . . . my parents had dropped off with the case worker."[21] He remembers how during this time he spent much time worrying about what the foster family thought of him and what was going to happen next.

Separation is difficult enough, but that is just the start of the foster care journey for a youth. Adjusting to a new family, new house, new rules, and possibly a new school is stressful. And for many in foster care, the separation and moves become a typical part of their lives.

Chapter 3

Creating a New Life

When foster kids talk about the system that places them with a new family, many call it *stranger care*, not *foster care*. The reason for this is clear: unless they are placed with relatives, they are moving in with absolute strangers. The experience can be daunting. After losing a hold on the only life they know, imperfect though it is, they must now try to build a new life with new people in a new and often unfamiliar place. Some, like Keily Orellana, are lucky. "In my foster home we are all a family," Orellana says. "When the food is ready we all eat together, we go out together, and sometimes my foster mom even takes us with her to different states to visit her family. She introduces us all as her grandchildren, and her daughters introduce us as their nieces or nephews."[22]

For other foster youth, adapting to a new family is a struggle. Not all foster parents understand what their foster children have been through. Or, in some cases, they just do not attempt to create any sort of bond between their foster kids and the rest of the family. When Shantae was placed with her foster family at the age of fifteen, she always felt like a burden. The family did not include her in any of their activities, such as game night or outings, and the biological daughter in the house often reminded her that she was not one of the family. Shantae ended up asking her social worker to take her out of the home.

> "In my foster home we are all a family."[22]
>
> —Keily Orellana, a foster youth.

New Rules, New Place

One of the first steps in adjusting to a new home is learning the rules. The youngsters have to adjust to the rules of the house if they are to get along with their foster parents. To start, they have to understand what is expected of them and what is not allowed. This can be a shock to young people who may be coming from homes where there was little parental oversight and few, or very different, rules. Some youth who enter foster care welcome the rules, having experienced only chaos in their own homes. Ashley Rivera is grateful for the rules and the support that her foster mother gives her. "[My foster mother] also treats her foster kids as if we were her own. If we do well in school she rewards us. If we do poorly, she punishes us,"[23] Rivera writes. Rivera's experience in foster care has given her the stability she desperately wanted.

The transition to a new home involves much more than unfamiliar rules. Foster youth often have no knowledge of the neighborhood where they are to live. For teens this can be especially troubling; not knowing where the local park or movie theater or burger place is can feel very alienating. Orellana has turned her experiences in foster care into an advice column for foster parents. She recommends that they help their foster youth get adjusted to the home and area first. "Introduce us to your home and neighborhood," Orellana advises. "We're often placed in a home far from where we used to live and it's hard to get around when we don't know where we are. Go out with us and show us where the stores, laundromats, transportation, and other important things are."[24] Just being made comfortable with their surroundings can ease a foster youth's transition.

> "We're often placed in a home far from where we used to live and it's hard to get around when we don't know where we are."[24]
>
> —Keily Orellana, a foster youth.

A teenage boy prepares to take out the trash. Foster youth must adjust to the rules and expectations they encounter in their new homes.

Adjusting to School

A big part of adapting to foster care is finding ways to fit in at a new school. A lot of foster kids are shunted from one family to another—which can mean adjusting to one new school after another. Every time they start a new school, they have to meet new

Abuse in Foster Care

Many foster parents are both caring and compassionate—but some are not. Abuse of foster children occurs in a small percentage of cases. One of these cases involved Lena Francis, who had been placed in foster care at birth. In 2014 Francis, then twenty, appeared before the Texas House Select Committee on Child Protection. The committee was investigating problems in Texas's foster care system after seven children died of abuse or neglect. Francis, who was adopted at age seven, described difficult years in foster care. She remembers that she was often locked in a dark room for hours and prohibited from eating or drinking. "These agencies, they don't know what happens," says Francis. "And how can you report that because, at the end of the day, you've still got to go home with that person?"

Quoted in Associated Press, "Tales of Foster Care Abuse in Texas Sound 'Like Prison,'" kxan.com, July 24, 2014. http://kxan.com.

teachers, find new friends, and learn their way around the school. And if they start in the middle of a semester, which is not uncommon, they have to figure out what to study and how to catch up with the rest of the students in their classes.

Ollie Hernandez understands the many difficulties of adjusting to a new school. She has had a lot of practice. She was in foster care from age nine to twelve, and then again from age thirteen to nineteen. Over the years she lived in several different homes and attended nine different schools. After every move she had to make new friends and get back into the routine of classes, studying, and tests.

Hernandez was dedicated to her education, but often it was hard to keep up. Every school seemed to have a different way of teaching the various subjects. What's more, her transcripts were always a few weeks behind her arrival at the new school, so she was often placed in classes either below or ahead of where she was supposed to be. When she got to high school, she finally had some stability—but it only lasted for three years. She had to start a new school in her senior year. It was a lonely, difficult period. "That really messed me up," she says. "It's hard to be in your senior year and not know anybody. I didn't try to talk to my peers who had normal upbringings and normal parents, and I didn't want favoritism from teachers. My idea was not to let anyone see me sweat,"[25] Hernandez says.

Coming from Behind

Because of the moves and other factors, foster kids have a high risk of falling behind in school. Studies have found that when a move to a new school happens, up to six months of academic progress can be lost. According to 2014 statistics released by the Formed Families Forward organization, students in foster care move schools at least once or twice a year, and by the time they age out of the system, over one-third will have experienced five or more school moves. As a result, studies have shown that foster youth have a high risk of dropping out of school and are unlikely to attend or graduate from college.

Those who are lucky enough to have a stable living situation with a caring foster family often end up doing better in school. Jimmy Wayne knows this from personal experience. Wayne entered foster care at age twelve and ended up attending twelve different schools. When he was in tenth grade, however, he was placed with a caring and stable foster family. Finally, he was able to adjust to

"It's hard to be in your senior year and not know anybody. I didn't try to talk to my peers who had normal upbringings and normal parents. . . . My idea was not to let anyone see me sweat."[25]

—Ollie Hernandez, a foster youth.

school and concentrate on his studies. "I don't even remember what I learned—no, let me rephrase that—I don't remember what they tried to teach me—after fifth grade," he says.

It wasn't until I had a stable home and was taken in by a loving family in tenth grade that I was able to hear anything, to *learn* anything. Before that, I wasn't thinking about science, I was thinking about what I was going to eat that day or where I could get clothes. When I was finally in one place for a while, going to the same school, everything changed. Even my handwriting improved. I could focus. I was finally able to learn.[26]

Friendship Trials

Moving to a new place means making new friends—or attempting to do so. For many foster youth, this is another difficult part of their lives. Some have trouble making friends because negative views of foster kids are common. Erica's foster care experiences gave her a firsthand view of biases against foster youth. "What is hard is when some children won't play with you because you are a foster child," Erica recalls. "There is still a stigma about being a foster child 'that we are all street kids' that I hope can eventually be broken."[27] At age seven Erica's father died and she was placed in a foster family. Then an older cousin decided she wanted to take care of her; after not getting along with her cousin, Erica was moved again. Each time she moved, she found it difficult to make friends because of the way other kids viewed her.

Other youngsters in foster care choose not to even try to make friends. Because they know that another move is possible—and even likely—many of them do not want to risk getting close to people.

> "What is hard is when some children won't play with you because you are a foster child."[27]
>
> —Erica, a foster youth.

As a group of youngsters chat, a teenage girl looks on. With each move, foster youth face the challenge of making new friends.

They cannot see the point of making a friend only to move and lose that friend—again. This leads some young people to isolate themselves from others. They develop a habit of keeping to themselves to avoid the possibility of getting to know someone who might only be in their lives for a short while.

Despite the worries about someday leaving, some youth do try to make friends. These efforts can be fraught with difficulty. Teens often act spontaneously—deciding at the last minute to hang out with a friend or drive with that friend to grab a burger or see a movie. For many teens, this would be a simple matter of checking in with their parents. It is a less-than-simple matter, however, for some teens in foster care. One youth recalls that his foster parents had to get permission from a caseworker for even simple requests such as: "Can I go hang out at a friend's house?" and "Can I ride with my friend?"[28] Making friends was not easy when faced with obstacles like this.

Navigating Relationships with Birth Parents

As if adjusting to a new home, new family, new school, and new friends were not challenging enough, most foster youth maintain relationships with their birth parent or parents. While in foster care most young people continue to see their parents in supervised visits. The most common arrangement is a weekly visit at the DCS office where parents and children spend about an hour together.

Some young people welcome these visits; others have no interest in seeing their parents but must go anyway. In both instances, conflicted feelings are common. It can be difficult to spend time, even an hour, with a parent who has been neglectful or abusive. It can also be painful to see a parent who is steadily self-destructing through drug or alcohol abuse. Sometimes young people hope to hear an apology that is not forthcoming. "What was weird to me at the time was even though I disliked my parents I still wanted them to like me," one former foster youth writes of his visits. "Even though I didn't want to go to the visit in the first place I still had that part of me that didn't want the visit to end because they hadn't yet said they would fix everything and or say sorry."[29]

And yet not all such visits are bad. Some young people feel joy to see their parents and then great sadness when they must leave them. Donisha remembers how happy she felt on her first visit with her mother; that visit and others always seemed too short. She recalls being told that first time that she would have two hours with her mother. "I was immediately enraged and said, 'What?! Two hours? That is not enough!'"[30]

Guilt is also an emotion that many youngsters feel when seeing their parents. Often a youth may be relieved to be living in a foster home that offers more in terms of safety, structure, comforts, and care than he or she had at home. The youth feels guilty for appreciating and enjoying this aspect of foster care. Many feel disloyal to their parents when they feel affection for their foster parents.

Adjusting to a Group Home

When a foster family cannot be found, which is more common for teens than for younger kids, the alternative is often a group home. Group homes provide care in an institutional setting. The typical group home has about six kids between the ages of twelve and eighteen and is staffed by live-in house parents. These adults provide guidance, structure, and support to the young people who live in the home. Group homes are typically more restrictive and regimented than family homes. Residents are assigned a shared room and are allotted a certain amount of space for personal belongings. Meals, chores, homework, and recreational time are often strictly regimented. Visitors and time for using the Internet or making phone calls are also tightly controlled.

Group home staff members are trained to deal with troubled young people, and many are dedicated to providing good-quality care, but they cannot always give the youths under their care what they want most: a sense of family. Staff members work in shifts, coming in at different hours, and kids move in and out, depending

Two teenagers play a video game. Because of the difficulty of placing older children with families, teens often end up living in group homes.

LGBTQ in Foster Care

Dealing with rejection as a foster youth is typical, but for teens who identify as LGBTQ (lesbian, gay, bisexual, transgender, queer or questioning), life in foster care can be even more troubling. Many of them report that they are scorned and ostracized. Authorities say it is difficult to find foster homes for them. Some foster families are not accepting of gay people. Many foster care agencies are faith-based organizations and recruit foster parents who share their religious views. "It's hard in general for adolescents to find homes," says Doug O'Dell, the chief program officer at Family of Services, a contracted foster care agency in New York City that has group homes specifically for LGBTQ youth. "It's really been difficult to find foster parents that themselves are LGBTQ or allies." For those who cannot find a home, group homes are their option. However, those who end up in group homes encounter other foster youth who bully them because of who they are. Efforts to find more foster parents who are LGBTQ or are accepting of LGBTQ youth continue in many parts of the country.

Quoted in Sarah Sugar, "Struggle Amid Progress: To Be LGBTQ in Foster Care," *City Limits*, July 16, 2014. http://citylimits.org.

on what is happening with their cases. Brandy Hernandez lived in two different group homes, and she did not have entirely negative experiences. The group home provided a therapist; being able to talk about her fears and concerns with this person was helpful. She also felt some relief at not having to constantly fear being kicked out of her home—which had happened when she lived with her mother. However, she did not feel her group homes provided an environment that youth crave. "Group homes should be a place where foster youth can grow up, feel like they belong and get help with their issues of being away from their families," she says. "But all they are is a place to sleep. A group home doesn't feel like a home."[31]

Living in a group home also makes it difficult to become independent because youth have little chance to make their own decisions. For example, they cannot choose when and where to meet friends, must get approval to join school activities, and are restricted as to what they can do during their free time. Jacque Mata-Lemons, who is now a college student, spent six years in a group home in Lubbock, Texas. She excelled at her schoolwork while there and was able to earn privileges due to following the rules and doing well in school, but she disliked the extensive restrictions and lack of personal relationships. With all the restrictions, she did not have the opportunity to make many decisions for herself. Anthony Robinson also stayed at a group home for two years and found that adjusting to an institutional setting means giving up independence, making it hard later. "It was hard to transition out," Robinson states. "But it's taught me that life is not always going to be like the [group home], where everything was given to me."[32]

What Works

Whether in a group home or a foster home, if a youth does not feel settled in and a sense of permanence, he or she will have a difficult time. Going day to day, unsure of what is going to happen next, is unsettling and does not provide the stability that foster care is meant to provide. The situations where foster care works is when the foster parent or parents are able to provide a sense of security that allows their young charges to adjust and live as normal a life as possible.

Manny was nine years old and in his third foster home before he finally began to feel safe and comfortable. His foster mother, Melba, gained Manny's trust over a period of months by being consistent with her rules and care, offering to help with homework, making meals every night, fulfilling any promises she made, and always being there for him. "I believed that Melba had paid her dues and earned her stripes as my foster mom. I started talking to Melba a lot, and I often found myself the one starting the conversations. We'd talk about the news, school, TV and anything else worth talking about,"[33] Manny explains.

After an initial period of adjustment, Manny was able to relax, grow, and thrive. His experiences reflect the hoped-for outcome of foster care.

Chapter 4

Exiting Foster Care

More than 250,000 young people exit the US foster care system every year. Of these, about 55 percent return to their parents. Another 20 percent are adopted. Most of the remaining youths will age out of the system. All three outcomes have their own set of challenges.

Edward Washington experienced the challenges of exiting the system firsthand. Washington, the oldest of twelve children, was born to a single mother who had left his heroin-addicted father. Because of neglect, he and his siblings entered foster care when Washington was fourteen. He lived in a group home where, overall, his experiences were positive. At age eighteen he started college and lived on campus. But when classes ended for the summer, Washington suddenly realized he had nowhere to go. "I tried going back to the group home, but I couldn't stay there because I had aged out," he says. "I hid out in my dorm until the school made me leave. I'd never felt so helpless."[34] That summer, Washington basically lived out of a plastic bag—carrying all his possessions with him wherever he went—staying on friends' couches and sometimes in parks. It was a scary and unsettling time. When classes started again in the fall, he moved back into campus housing and made plans to stay with friends during subsequent summer breaks. For Washington, exiting the foster care system proved difficult and made him feel helpless; many others exiting the system, whether through aging out, reunification, or adoption, experience similar feelings.

Reunification

In most cases reunification between parents and children lasts, but sometimes it does not. Reunification can occur only after parents demonstrate to social workers that they can provide a safe, stable home environment for their children and that they are regularly attending any required programs such as for drug addiction and improving parenting skills.

The process begins with parents and children meeting for supervised visits every week or so. Typically, they meet at a DCS office to talk and share what is going on in their lives. Eventually, parents and children progress to hour-long unsupervised visits and then to overnight visits. The goal of these visits is to help parents and children reconnect before they actually move back in together as a family.

When the DCS feels that both the youth and parents are ready, they are reunited in the hope that this arrangement will last. It did for Leah and her mother, although not right away. Leah became a foster child at age nine. Her mother, Donna, had battled depression and drug abuse and had attempted suicide more than once. Because of these problems, Donna's parental rights were terminated and Leah was placed in foster care. In her teen years, Leah discovered where her mother was living and visited her. By

A young man sleeps on a couch. Foster youth who age out of the system often find themselves homeless.

this time Donna had dealt with her depression and drug abuse and was living a stable life.

When Leah's caseworker found out about these visits, she investigated the situation and listened to Leah's wishes. The caseworker decided that since Leah and her mother were bonding, she would try to help them reunite as a family. The caseworker developed a plan that consisted of rebuilding the mother-daughter relationship, first through supervised and then through unsupervised visits. With help from a nonprofit organization, the two attended a wilderness camp where they learned techniques for dealing with each other on a variety of issues. After this camp they reunited for good, and both are satisfied with the results. Leah continues to live at home and is now a freshman at cosmetology school. "I am a successful person because I am doing what I want to do in my life, and I'm happy with it,"[35] says Leah.

Mixed Emotions

Many youngsters in foster care have mixed feelings about reuniting with their parents. After months or years of separation and upheaval, some have difficulty accepting the idea of once again living with their parents. Others might be happy about the idea of it but still worry that the changes their parents have made will not last and that things will go back to the way they were. Furthermore, foster youth who have grown close to their foster families and new friends and have adapted to a new school might resent having to leave all of that behind.

Brunilda Rivera and her son, Brandon, have experienced a rocky reunification. Brandon was placed in foster care after his mother was ordered to serve an eighteen-month jail sentence for drug-related charges. In prison, Rivera dedicated herself to becoming a better mother. She worked with a drug addiction program to become sober. Likewise, with help from the New York City DCS, she got a job and arranged for a place to live once she was released. She and Brandon were reunited, but the reunification was not easy. Brandon was bitter and resentful; he felt his mother had abandoned him. "He was angry and sometimes right now he's still angry," Rivera says. "He would kick me, and

Extended to Twenty-One?

Being on your own at age eighteen with no support is a frightening prospect. More than half of the states agree and are providing funding for youth to stay in foster care until age twenty-one, if they choose to. States can do this since the Fostering Connections to Success and Increasing Adoptions Act of 2008 was enacted. This federal law allows states to use federal foster care money for eligible youths up to age twenty-one, rather than eighteen. Both anecdotal reports and statistics support the fact that keeping young people in foster care until twenty-one increases the chance of successful independence. A University of Chicago study followed a group of young people from Illinois, Iowa, and Wisconsin as they aged out of foster care and transitioned to adulthood. The study found that young people who remain in care until twenty-one tend to have better outcomes than young people who leave care at eighteen. "We've really seen youth take advantage of the opportunity to stay in care, to get continued resources, to make the transition to adulthood a little smoother," says Jennifer Rodriguez, a former foster care youth who is now the executive director of the Youth Law Center in San Francisco.

Teresa Wiltz, "States Tackle 'Aging Out' of Foster Care," *Bend (OR) Bulletin*, March 31, 2015. www .bendbulletin.com.

hit me and he just didn't know how to show his feelings."[36] In the years following their reunification, mother and son have attended individual counseling and family therapy sessions together. These helped them learn to communicate in a positive manner, and Brandon's trust in his mother has begun to grow.

A successful reunification can only occur if the parents recognize that they need to rebuild their relationship and prove to their children that they can be trusted. "Separation hurts the trust between a parent and a child," explains Tanya Krupat, program director for the Osborne Association's New York Initiative for Children of Incarcerated Parents. "Once a child has experienced that separation, the fear that the parent will disappear again is also great."[37] The reunification process can be a long road but ultimately a satisfying one for the family if the relationships are rebuilt.

Failed Reunifications

Unfortunately, there are many examples of families that reunited and then fell apart again. National data from the 2014 US Department of Health and Human Services Outcomes Report indicates that 11.8 percent of youngsters who were reunited with parents reentered foster care within twelve months of the family getting back together. The problem in many cases is that parents fall back into their old patterns.

Jennifer Gibson describes what happened when she and her two sisters were returned to their mother. The mother had stopped doing drugs and seemed to have her life back on track. Gibson and her sisters, who had been living in separate foster homes, all moved back into the house with their mother. For the first few months all went well, but it did not last. Their mother started doing drugs again. "Eventually, we were back to only eating at school, nothing in the refrigerator," Gibson recalls. "My mother was back to using drugs and we'd moved to three schools in one year. I remember many nights waiting for my mom to come home, many times wondering if she would come home and pack us up so we could move again. Her cycle of drug use and rotten boyfriends had come back full swing."[38] Gibson and her sisters returned to foster care.

Failed reunifications further erode a young person's ability to trust others. A youth who has undergone a failed reunification finds it more difficult to develop relationships with others, particu-

> "Once a child has experienced that separation, the fear that the parent will disappear again is also great."[37]
>
> —Tanya Krupat, program director for the Osborne Association's New York Initiative for Children of Incarcerated Parents.

larly parental figures. Some youngsters deal with their disappointment and sadness by acting out to avoid getting close to people. And, after the time spent at home, their chances of being reunified again, or adopted, are significantly reduced.

Adoption

Many youths in foster care will never be returned to their biological parents. About 21 percent of the young people who exited foster care in 2014 were adopted by another family. Most of these are younger children. The majority of foster youth who are adopted are under age seven, according to the North American Council on Adoptable Children. With 43 percent of waiting children aged nine or older, this leaves many youngsters with a small prospect of a forever home. Despite these odds, many still hope.

Of those waiting for adoption, just over 50 percent are adopted by their foster parents. This leads to an easier transition than if they were adopted by another family because they already have developed a relationship with their foster parents. At age

Two children do their homework as their adoptive mother looks on. Twenty percent of foster youth are eventually adopted.

Always Hope

Davion was a youth that many assumed would age out of the system, never to find a family. At age sixteen he made a public plea at his church for someone to adopt him after he had been through twenty foster homes. Having grown up in the system, Davion had many issues to deal with, and though people responded to his plea, they did not work out because of personality issues. But on April 22, 2015, his caseworker, Connie Going, who had known him since he was just seven years old, officially adopted him as her son. "I never unpacked my bags throughout my life because I always knew I would have to leave," Davion says. "But after I was finalized, I had a lot of relief. I now know that this bed and room is mine. No one can take it away from me." He now has siblings, one who is Connie Going's biological child and another who was also adopted. Davion beat the odds—adopted out of foster care as a teen. He gives other young people hope that a forever family, even as an older youth, is not impossible.

Jennifer Ludden, "Helping Foster Kids Even After Adoption," NPR, August 28, 2012. www.npr.org.

six, Michael and his sister were placed with a single mother and her nine-year-old son. They bonded well, and Michael felt safe. "One day, she sat us down and asked if we'd like to join the family," Michael remembers. "It was so easy to say yes."[39] With his new mom's encouragement, Michael went on to play the guitar and sports, attend college, and enter the Marine Corps, a lifelong dream. For Michael, adoption by his foster mom provided the stability he needed.

Adapting to a New Family

Adoption from a family other than the foster family can be more challenging. Young people must adjust to the idea that they are with a permanent family who is completely new to them, after months or even years of instability. Additionally, it can be hard to adjust to new rules and a new household. As a result, many youngsters, after adoption, display behavioral problems.

Behavioral problems are the result of distrust and disbelief that they have found a permanent home. Phillip was nine when Carlton Hadden and Ronnie Roebuck adopted him. He had already been through ten foster care placements and two failed adoptions. He desperately wanted to be adopted, but he had difficulty dealing with it actually happening. Phillip, who acted out often during those days, told his new parents at the time, "I have major issues."[40] Typical ways that youth act out are talking back, refusing to obey parents and other authority issues, and skipping school.

These issues do not just resolve themselves. Successful adoption of youth, particularly older ones, occurs when the parents get help with the transition. To help Phillip and themselves adjust to the adoption, Roebuck says they immediately started individual therapy for Phillip and family therapy for all of them. Without this help, Roebuck says, they would not have succeeded; but with it, at age thirteen Phillip is no longer acting out. And, for the first time that anyone can recall, he is even excited about school.

> "One day, [my foster mother] sat us down and asked if we'd like to join the family. It was so easy to say yes."[39]
>
> —Michael, an adopted foster youth.

Aging Out

Foster youth who are not adopted or sent back to their families eventually age out of the foster care system at age eighteen. For most eighteen-year-olds, they start out on a road to independence gradually, either moving to college or into an apartment while working at a job, but still with parents who provide guidance and emotional and financial support. Eighteen-year-olds who exit foster care are primarily on their own from the day they leave the system. Often, because of their unstable upbringing, these young adults are more at risk for failure; many lack the basic skills needed to look after themselves.

Of the 238,230 youths who exited foster care in 2014, a total of 22,392 aged out of the system. These young adults must find a job and housing. They must learn to shop for food and other necessities, cook, clean, budget their money, and more. And they must do all of this without the support of parents or other relatives. The shock of this change, even for young people who are used to living with instability and constant change, can be overwhelming. "I live on my own now; it's a little weird. I'm trying to get used to it. You get lonely and stuff. You got nobody else to talk to,"[41] says Josh Mendoza, a former foster youth in Florida who aged out at eighteen and now is working toward his general equivalency diploma (GED).

Preparation

Before a foster youth ages out, the DCS tries to provide some preparation for what lies ahead. Foster youth nearing age eighteen take part in classes that teach budgeting; general life skills, such as how to balance a checkbook and pay bills; and how to search for a job and an apartment. They are also introduced to educational opportunities and how to get government financial help. In some states the DCS helps foster youth set up an initial place to stay and find a job, but after age eighteen the relationship ends. The youth may still receive financial support from the government, but no guidance or emotional support. Shawn Denise Semelsberger aged out of foster care at eighteen and felt totally unprepared for life on her own. "When I graduated from high school, I could not afford to buy a cap and gown, so I didn't walk with my class. I never purchased a yearbook, because I couldn't afford it. Worse yet, I had nobody to teach me how to grocery shop, cook, or balance a checkbook. At 22, I am still learning how,"[42] writes Semelsberger.

> "I had nobody to teach me how to grocery shop, cook, or balance a checkbook."[42]
>
> —Shawn Denise Semelsberger, an aged-out foster youth.

Some young people, though not the majority, do receive help even after they leave foster care. Josh Mendoza is one of

A young woman shops for juice in a supermarket. Youth who age out of the foster care system must learn how to live independently.

these. He continues to receive help from a nonprofit organization, Camelot Community Care, after having exited foster care. Nick Reschke is his transition specialist, which is someone who helps those exiting foster care. Even with Reschke's help, it is still a difficult transition. "The day he turned 18, we went to pick up his check, went grocery shopping, went over a list of what he needs, what his budgets are," says Reschke, who also helped Mendoza pick up some donated furniture and supplies. "And then after that, Josh and I, we pretty much just cleaned the apartment up, wiped down the counters, wiped down the cabinets and set up his house. And that was his first night."[43]

Aging-Out Impacts

The statistics for teens who age out of foster care are not promising. Forty to 50 percent of these young people become homeless within eighteen months, according to the Cities Counties Schools Partnership. Kristopher Sharp became one of these statistics after he aged out of the Texas foster care system. Sharp had basically grown up in foster care, having lived in twenty different homes throughout his childhood. Soon after aging out, he ended up living on the streets.

Sharp says that the fact he is gay made it more difficult to find shelter because he found that many residents in homeless shelters were hostile to gay people. He often ended up sleeping in parks and other places outdoors. "My life was reduced to two sets of clothes, a well-worn backpack and the streets. By day, I begged strangers for change; by night, I was turning tricks for a place to stay, a shower, a hot meal or whatever resources I could trade my body for," Sharp says. "That was my reality."[44] After six months of living on the streets, Sharp discovered that Texas offers free college tuition at state colleges to those who age out of foster care. With this help, Sharp was able to attend college. Once at college, he also was able to apply for financial aid; when he received his first check, he used it to rent an apartment and end his homelessness.

Avoiding homelessness is just one challenge foster youth face when they age out of the system. Another is getting an education. According to Foster Care to Success, a nonprofit organization

"My life was reduced to two sets of clothes, a well-worn backpack and the streets. By day, I begged strangers for change."[44]

—Kristopher Sharp, a formerly homeless foster youth.

that helps former foster youth, fewer than 10 percent of US foster youths graduate from college. By age twenty-six, only 80 percent of young people who aged out of foster care earned at least a high school degree or GED compared to 94 percent in the general population. Other problems that foster youth encounter are drugs, jail time, and teenage pregnancies. All of these outcomes are more likely for those who age out of foster care than for those who grow up with a stable home life.

Moving Forward

No matter what the outcome, former foster youth deal with loss the rest of their lives. All experience disrupted lives, and many also deal with some sort of trauma in connection with their biological or foster parents. Whether adopted, reunited, or aged out, these young people must find a way to move forward.

Chapter 5

Improving Foster Care

The foster care system is a safety net. It was created to provide safe, stable, temporary homes for neglected or abused young people. Like all safety nets, it catches some of the youngsters in need but misses others. Sometimes, even those it catches end up hurt. For these reasons, legislators, government agencies, nongovernmental organizations, and interested members of the public are trying to improve the system and even develop new ways of helping kids in need.

Reducing the Need for Foster Care

A major effort is under way to reduce the need for foster care. Studies show that youth do better when they are able to remain with their parents (even troubled parents), provided the home environment can be made safe. Therefore, many states are developing programs that focus on getting parents the help they need *before* their children are placed in foster care. Oklahoma, for example, focuses on the fact that neglect, rather than abuse, is the most common reason for placing youth in foster care. Neglect is somewhat easier to address than abuse; parents can be taught how to provide healthy meals and keep their houses clean, for example. "The majority of these children were placed in foster care as a result of neglect, not physical or sexual abuse," says Deborah Smith of the Oklahoma Department of Human Services. "A recent study of this issue revealed that many of these children could have safely stayed in their homes had more intensive, home-based services been available to their families."[45]

In response to this study, Oklahoma has enacted programs that teach parents basic skills such as cooking, cleaning, and time management so that their children get to school and appointments on time. If a child is found to be living in filth, agencies contracted with the state will show the parents how to clean and organize their house rather than immediately place the child in foster care. The Oklahoma agency believes that this approach will result in more children remaining with their families and getting needed help without the pain of separation.

Another program aimed at preventing the separation of families is New York City's Keeping Families Together program. This program provides housing and services such as job search assistance, substance abuse help, and parenting classes to families experiencing homelessness. Children in homeless families often end up in foster care. To determine whether this program is working, twenty-nine participating New York City families were tracked from October 2007 to July 2009. Upon entering the program, these families were all the subject of several ongoing child welfare cases involving maltreatment and/or neglect of the children. The program found that more than half of the cases were favorably resolved during the families' involvement with Keeping Families Together.

Mounds of dirty dishes wait for someone to wash them. Many states are trying to reduce the need for foster homes by teaching neglectful parents to take better care of their children.

Many young people who have lived in foster care support these types of programs. Mary Lee, a former foster care youth, writes that getting families help in hopes of allowing them to remain together is worthwhile. "Many of us could avoid foster care if the right help were provided to our parents. Intensive services that strengthen and restore struggling families can keep children out of foster care entirely," Lee explains. "That's best for most kids—and society."[46]

Decreasing Time in Limbo

Although most authorities agree that keeping families together is ideal, they acknowledge that this is not always possible. In the instances when foster care is necessary, the goal is to reduce the amount of time young people spend in the system. According to the July 2015 AFCARS report, youngsters typically spend about nineteen months in foster care. And some spend much more than that; there are many cases of young people in and out of foster care for years at a time. All agree that this is not a good situation. Once youngsters are in foster care, the goal is to return them to their own home as soon as it is considered safe or to find a family to adopt them. Many states have laws that require a decision within twelve months of a youth's being taken from the home. This means the state must officially determine whether the goal for the youth is reunification, adoption, or independence within a year. Once a goal is in place, the caseworkers can work toward achieving this goal (and decreasing the youth's time in foster care).

"Many of us could avoid foster care if the right help were provided to our parents."[46]

—Mary Lee, a former foster youth.

Another law enacted to decrease youths' time in foster care is the 1997 Adoption and Safe Families Act. This act requires that, where possible, states move to terminate parental rights for children who have been in foster care for fifteen out of the last twenty-

Trying to Stay Healthy

When a person knows that he or she can afford to go to a doctor if sick, it is a major relief. For years, foster youth who aged out of the system automatically lost their health care coverage and hoped they did not get sick or have an accident. The Affordable Health Care Act of 2014 changed this, and now Medicaid coverage is provided for former foster youth until they reach age twenty-six. However, there is one downside: this is only applicable if the youth remains in the state where he or she was in foster care. Still, for most aged-out youth, it provides a safety net and gives them the assistance that they need.

two months. The purpose of this rule is to encourage states to work toward reuniting youngsters with their parents or move toward adoption. Although some say these rules help young people to exit foster care in a timely manner, others say the rules are often disregarded. Agencies and courts are able to use loopholes to ignore the rules, causing painful delays for children. Still others say the rules are too rigid and do not allow enough time for parents to get their lives on track. "Whenever you're talking about child welfare, having something that has these very rigid timelines, that doesn't take individual circumstances into consideration, is a problem,"[47] says Philip Gentry, a Columbia Law School professor and the leading national authority on incarcerated parents. For example, Gentry says, it has become common for incarcerated mothers to lose their parental rights because they do not have enough time to serve their prison sentence and meet the requirements to gain their children back.

Maintaining Consistency

The government is also trying to improve educational consistency for foster youth. Foster youth deal with a multitude of educational issues, and without consistency their difficulties increase. For example, many of these kids have learning disabilities or other problems that require individual education plans (IEPs) at school. An IEP defines the individualized objectives of a child who has been found to have a learning disability. It also may require certain accommodations, such as having tests read to them or extra time to accomplish tasks, to help them meet overall education goals. Making sure important records like IEPs follow youngsters from one school to the next can be difficult—especially because foster youth are forced to move and change schools so often. In fact, 32 percent of students in foster care change schools in a given year, compared to 7 percent of students as a whole. It is not uncommon for school records to take weeks or even months to reach the new school.

By the time a youth's records arrive, he or she is already starting to fall behind without the necessary special help. This affects the youth's overall education and contributes to the drop-out rate

Students take notes in a classroom. Foster youth often fall behind academically because they change schools frequently.

for foster youth. According to the National Working Group on Foster Care and Education, only half of all teens in foster care complete high school by their eighteenth birthday, compared to 70 percent for teens not in the foster care system.

Federal laws passed in 2008 and 2013 attempt to remedy this situation. The Fostering Connections to Success and Increasing Adoptions Act of 2008 and the Uninterrupted Scholars Act of 2013 ensure that social workers have timely access to school records of foster youth. Before, caseworkers had to obtain special permission from courts or biological parents to obtain school records. Schools may now release a youth's education records to a caseworker without the written permission of a parent.

Even with these laws, foster youth are not always able to maintain school consistency. Although the law requires the social worker to attempt to keep a youth at his or her current school during placement, sometimes a new foster home is too far away for this to be possible. This happened to Octavia Lacks. Lacks entered foster care during ninth grade and moved in and out of eleven homes in three years, changing schools five times. In the process, she found that some of the classes she had taken elsewhere did not count toward the next school's required graduation credits. When this happens, students may have to retake courses, causing them to fall further behind. "When I transferred between school districts, the credits I had didn't always transfer, and the credits I had at one school didn't always count at other schools,"[48] says Lacks.

Giving Youth a Voice

Often, foster youth feel they have no say in their future. At best, they are told what is happening with their case, but they are unable to say what they want. At worst, they are moved to new places without any explanation or warning. With all of the changes, they also feel that no one person is always there for them. In response, programs are now in place that help to make their voices heard.

A national program that empowers foster youth is the Court Appointed Special Advocates (CASA). This organization provides volunteers who are appointed by judges to advocate for abused and neglected children and ensure that the youth do not get lost in the legal and social service system. Often, youth complain that they do not see their caseworker enough or their caseworker keeps changing; as a result, they do not understand what decisions are being made in court regarding their lives. They long for someone who will provide them with information and listen to them. CASA volunteers fill this role by establishing and maintaining a relationship with a youth until he or she is in a permanent home; they also ensure that the youth is aware, understands, and has a voice in decisions directly affecting his or her life. Typically, a CASA volunteer attends all of the youth's court proceedings on foster care, school, and any related issue. The CASA advocate reads through all of the relevant paperwork, talks to the youth on a regular basis, speaks for the youth in court, recommends services for the youth and his or her family based on the advocate's observations, and ensures that the youth totally understands all that is occurring.

"[My CASA volunteer] was the anchor I desperately needed to stay in school, to keep moving forward."[49]

—Laura, a former foster youth.

At age twelve, Laura entered foster care after being first abused by her father, then suffering neglect as her mother struggled with mental illness. She spent five years in foster care and had more than a dozen social workers during that time. At every court date in which her future was being decided, she had a new lawyer. However, she had one consistent person in her life: her CASA volunteer, Sally Payne. "Knowing Sally cared about me meant the world to me. She was the anchor I desperately needed to stay in school, to keep moving forward, to make the choices that got me safely out of foster care and into service to my country,"[49] says Laura, who, after exiting foster care, served in the Marine Corps and is now a police officer.

A young woman meets with a volunteer from Court Appointed Special Advocates (CASA) and a social worker. CASA volunteers work to ensure that foster youth receive needed services and understand what is being done on their behalf.

Preparing for Independence

Preparing youth for life after foster care is another important area being addressed. The average eighteen-year-old is unprepared for life as a fully independent person. For eighteen-year-olds coming out of foster care, the challenge is much greater. They typically have little or no emotional, educational, or monetary support. Foster youth are often handicapped by a lack of education and life skills.

State agencies and nonprofit organizations are attempting to make this transition smoother for foster youth who age out. When a youth is within a few years of aging out of foster care, even if there is still a possibility of adoption, the DCS is supposed to help the youth plan for independence. In the best case scenario, the DCS provides the youth with life skills classes, helps the youth set up housing and a job and/or school, and ensures that the youth understands what government help, such as health insurance and educational grants, are available to them. The problem is that not every youth receives all or even any of these services. Chris was taken by surprise when he learned that he had to leave foster care, recalling that "two weeks before my high school graduation,

Being Heard

Often foster youth complain that their input is not heard, and they are not made aware of all that is going on in their cases. Children's Rights, a nonprofit organization dedicated to protecting the rights of youth, filed a suit in Atlanta, Georgia, in 2002 to improve this situation in the counties of metropolitan Atlanta. At the time there were only two attorneys in DeKalb County specializing in representing youth in situations involving foster care, neglect, and abuse, and each carried caseloads for as many as five hundred children. Similarly, Fulton County youth attorneys had an average of four hundred cases apiece in 2002. As a result, youth who faced life-altering court decisions—such as where they would live and whether they could be returned home to their parents—generally did not receive updated communications, and their attorneys neither had a detailed understanding of their cases nor knew what was in their best interest.

The Children's Rights suit resulted in significant reforms within Atlanta. By 2008, eleven attorneys were dedicated to the youth cases of DeKalb, with caseloads of fewer than one hundred each; in Fulton County, the caseloads were reduced to sixty-three children per lawyer by 2010. This enables each attorney to better represent and communicate with each youth. Children's Rights has filed and closed cases in other states, such as Michigan and Rhode Island, to reform the way foster youth are represented.

they told me I had to leave. I couldn't believe it, I asked them, 'Are you serious?' And they were."[50]

States are attempting to provide foster youth like Chris with better transition services. Federal programs such as the John H. Chafee Foster Care Independence Program and the Educational and Training Vouchers (ETV) Program for Youths Aging Out of Foster Care are providing grants and assistance to states so that they might better assist foster youth. The Chafee program provides funding for states to set up transitional housing services for youth. The ETV program authorized $60 million for payments to states for postsecondary education and training vouchers for foster youth who are leaving the system.

Specifically, states are using funding to create independent living skills programs (ILSPs) to help foster youth become independent as they exit foster care. These programs include résumé and financial aid workshops and education, housing, and job assistance. Many ILSPs also offer a library and lounge area for emancipated youth to meet one another. States are also using the funding to implement other programs to help prepare youth. In Michigan, for example, the state has implemented a Big Brothers/Big Sisters program that provides mentors to older youth as they become independent. "I believe it's essential that students from foster care have supportive adults in their lives, people they can really rely upon as they exit care,"[51] says Jason Sides, the coordinator of the Michigan Youth Opportunities Initiative for the Michigan Department of Health and Human Services.

> "Two weeks before my high school graduation, they told me I had to leave. I couldn't believe it, I asked them, 'Are you serious?' And they were."[50]
>
> —Chris, a former foster youth.

Establishing Relationships

Many who age out of foster care, and even those who have been reunited or adopted after foster care, long for emotional support from someone who understands what they have experienced. A variety of nonprofit organizations help those exiting foster care by providing housing and education services and emotional support. Many organizations accomplish this through the alumni programs that connect former foster youth. Heart 2 Heart in Fairfield, California, brings former foster youth together throughout the year with parties and gatherings so they can establish relationships and find support. "All of the people here are like a family,"[52] says Griffin, a former foster care youth who now volunteers at Heart 2 Heart. Additionally, Heart 2 Heart provides items such as clothes, house supplies, and school supplies to youth who are now on their own. The organization also connects youth with programs that can help them pay for higher education and with adult volunteers who can offer advice on matters including education, housing, and life issues.

The Future

Improvements to the foster care system, both from inside and outside the system, are essential to protecting youth and ensuring they have the ability and opportunity to set and achieve their goals. Greta Anderson credits both foster care and organizations dedicated to helping foster youth to her becoming an independent, grounded adult. Anderson lived in foster care for two years and experienced six different placements in addition to being separated from her sister before aging out. Because she had help from individuals and various organizations, she is now a senior majoring in art education at the University of Wisconsin–Stout. She also has served as an intern with the FosterClub and the National Resource Center for Youth Development, both organizations dedicated to helping foster youth. After her own experiences, she believes that if more people get involved and give of themselves, the system can improve and offer youth what they need. To Anderson, foster care "is something that gives me perspective on a population that often goes unseen. Older youths in foster care experience unique challenges in transitioning, and people in

> "Older youths in foster care experience unique challenges in transitioning, and people in every occupation and life situation can contribute to improving our chances for success."[53]
>
> —Greta Anderson, a former foster youth.

every occupation and life situation can contribute to improving our chances for success."[53]

The foster care system works to provide safety and stability to young people and their families. It is a difficult task as children who enter foster care have already suffered and need to be taken care of not only physically but also emotionally. Improvements to the system are continually being made to ensure that youth receive the physical, emotional, and mental care required for a stable childhood. Every youth deserves a family and to grow in a safe environment.

Source Notes

Introduction: Traumatic Beginnings

1. Quoted in Sarah Favot, "For One Foster Teen, Years of Change, and Then a Forever Home," *Los Angeles Daily News*, December 24, 2014. www.dailynews.com.
2. Lisa Basile, "Foster Care Youth: We Are Everyone & No One's Responsibility," *Huffington Post*, May 19, 2015. www.huffingtonpost.com.

Chapter 1: The Foster Care System

3. Quoted in Sophie Quinton, "How Heroin Is Hitting the Foster Care System," Pew Charitable Trusts, October 9, 2015. www.pewtrusts.org.
4. Quoted in Emily Bregel, "Parental Substance Abuse Main Reason Kids End Up in Foster Care," *Arizona Daily Star* (Tucson), December 9, 2013. http://tucson.com.
5. Quoted in Dylan McCoy, "Growing Need for Foster Parents Strains Region," *Lafayette (IN) Journal & Courier*, September 26, 2015. www.jconline.com.
6. Janelle A., "A Difficult Journey Home," *Connection*, Fall 2008. www.casaforchildren.org.
7. Quoted in Erin Robertson, "Former Foster Child Defies Odds, Heads to UCLA on Full-Ride Scholarship," Root, June 17, 2014. www.theroot.com.

Chapter 2: Removal

8. Basile, "Foster Care Youth."
9. Jamie Schwandt and Amber Beach Hardacre, "Dreaming Big! Success in Kansas Foster Care," *Hays (KS) Post*, May 19, 2015. www.hayspost.com.
10. Quoted in Nikky Greer, "Heather, a Fostered Youth," My Foster Care Story, November 19, 2014. http://myfostercarestory.com.

11. Anonymous, "They're All I Have," L.A. Youth, May 2011. www
.layouth.com.
12. Quoted in Davina A. Merritt, *Fostering Hope for America*. San
Bernardino, CA: CreateSpace, 2014.
13. Campbell, "Moving Foster Homes," *Percolated Paradox* (blog),
November 4, 2010. http://percolatedparadox.blogspot.com.
14. Briana, "Pseudo Lockdown," Children's Rights, 2014. www
.childrensrights.org.
15. Quoted in *Fostering Perspectives*, "Honoring and Maintaining Sibling Connections," November 2009. www.fosteringper
spectives.org.
16. Yaya, "Building the Strength to Speak Up," Children's Rights,
2014. www.childrensrights.org.
17. Quoted in David Hoffman, "Michelle Became a Foster Kid at
9," YouTube, May 9, 2012. www.youtube.com.
18. Dylan McIntosh, "Instability," Children's Rights, 2014. www
.childrensrights.org.
19. Quoted in Hope Redeemed Ministries blog, "A Broken System," July 22, 2014. https://hoperedeemedministries.word
press.com.
20. Quoted in CBS 5, "DCS Addresses Why Foster Kids Are
Sleeping in State Office Buildings," October 25, 2014. www
.cbs5az.com.
21. Anonymous, "What It's Like to Be a Foster Care Child," ImA
Foster.com, January 2012. www.imafoster.com.

Chapter 3: Creating a New Life

22. Keily Orellana, "Simple Tips for Foster Parents," YouthSuc-
cessNYC, 2014. www.youthsuccessnyc.org.
23. Ashley Rivera, "My Mother Is a Role Model," YouthSuccess-
NYC, 2014. www.youthsuccessnyc.org.
24. Orellana, "Simple Tips for Foster Parents."
25. Quoted in Annie E. Casey Foundation, "Foster Youth Share
Their School Experiences," January 28, 2014. www.fostercare
andeducation.org.
26. Quoted in Jessica Lahey, "Every Time Foster Kids Move, They
Lose Months of Academic Progress," *Atlantic*, February 28,
2014. www.theatlantic.com.

27. Quoted in Fostering NSW, "Erica—Foster Child." http://fos teringnsw.com.au.

28. Anonymous, "How to Get Your Kids Out of Foster Care," ImA Foster.com, 2015. www.imafoster.com.

29. Anonymous, "How to Get Your Kids Out of Foster Care."

30. Donisha, "My Experience with Visits," *Fostering Perspectives*, November 2010. www.fosteringperspectives.org.

31. Brandy Hernandez, "You Call This Home?," L.A. Youth, October 2007. www.layouth.com.

32. Quoted in David Crary, "Foster Care: US Moves to Phase Out Group Care for Foster Kids," *Christian Science Monitor*, May 2014. www.csmonitor.com.

33. Quoted in Sophia Williams-Baugh, "They Don't Know the Life of a Foster Care Child," *Huffington Post*, September 22, 2014. www.huffingtonpost.com.

Chapter 4: Exiting Foster Care

34. Quoted in Cynthia Gordy, "The Root: Helping Foster Care Kids After They Leave," NPR, May 10, 2011. www.npr.org.

35. Quoted in Annie E. Casey Foundation, "Reunification and Lifelong Families, a Foster Care Practice Model," November 13, 2012. www.youtube.com.

36. Quoted in Lily Vosoughi, "Family Ties: The Fight to Reunite Families After Incarceration," Women Out of Prison, 2010. https://nyunewsdoc.wordpress.com.

37. Quoted in Vosoughi, "Family Ties."

38. Jennifer Gibson, "What Might Have Been," FosterClub, 2015. www.fosterclub.com.

39. Quoted in Adopt US Kids, "Dreams Realized," 2016. www .adoptuskids.org.

40. Quoted in Jennifer Ludden, "Helping Foster Kids After Adoption," NPR, August 28, 2012. www.npr.org.

41. Quoted in Pam Fessler, "Foster Kids Face Tough Times After 18," NPR, April 7, 2010. www.npr.org.

42. Shawn Denise Semelsberger, "Foster Youth Who 'Age Out' Are Forced to Become Adults Before They Are Ready," Foster-Club, 2015. www.fosterclub.com.

43. Fessler, "Foster Kids Face Tough Times After 18."

44. Kristopher Sharp, "Falling Through the Cracks: My Struggle to Survive as a Homeless Youth," *POZ*, July/August 2015. www.poz.com.

Chapter 5: Improving Foster Care

45. Quoted in *Ada (OK) News*, "DHS Receives Approval to Launch Efforts to Reduce Need for Foster Care, Recruit Adoptive Families," October 10, 2014. www.theadanews.com.
46. Mary Lee, "Six Things You Should Know About Growing Up in Foster Care," *Huffington Post*, June 17, 2015. www.huff ingtonpost.com.
47. Quoted in Sharona Coutts and Zoe Greenberg, "'No Hope for Me': Women Stripped of Parental Rights After Minor Crimes," *RH Reality Check*, April 2, 2015. http://rhrealitycheck.org.
48. Quoted in Annie E. Casey Foundation, "Foster Youth Share Their School Experiences," January 28, 2014. www.aecf.org.
49. Laura, "Laura's Story," CASA, 2015. www.casaforchildren .org.
50. Quoted in FosterClub, "Leaving Foster Care on His Own," 2015. www.fosterclub.com.
51. Quoted in Deb Pascoe, "How Michigan Foster Youths Are Transitioning to Adulthood Successfully," Upper Peninsula Second Wave, October 28, 2015. http://up.secondwavemedia.com.
52. Quoted in Ian Thompson, "Heart 2 Heart Reaches Out to Former Foster Care Youth," *Fairfield-Suisun (CA) Daily Republic*, March 8, 2015. www.dailyrepublic.com.
53. Greta Anderson, "One State Foster Kid's Story," *Milwaukee Journal Sentinel*, 2015. www.jsonline.com.

Annie E. Casey Foundation

701 St. Paul St.
Baltimore, MD 21202
phone: (410) 547-6600
website: www.aecf.org

This organization focuses on improving the well-being of American youth. Its goal is to build better futures for disadvantaged children and their families. One focus is to improve the child welfare system and improve the lives of foster youth.

Children's Bureau

1250 Maryland Ave. SW, 8th Floor
Washington, DC 20024
website: www.acf.hhs.gov/programs/cb

The Children's Bureau is a federal agency that partners with federal, state, tribal, and local agencies to improve the overall health and well-being of children and families in the United States. This includes foster care and protection of abused and neglected youth.

Children's Rights

330 Seventh Ave., 4th Floor
New York, NY 10001
phone: (212) 683-2210
website: www.childrensrights.org

This organization is dedicated to protecting the rights of abused and neglected youth and giving them a voice. Children's Rights uses the law to hold the government accountable, and it defends thousands of kids when foster care systems fail.

Court Appointed Special Advocates for Children (CASA)

529 Fourteenth St. NW, Suite 420
Washington, DC 20045
phone: (800) 628-3233
website: www.casaforchildren.org

This national organization supports and promotes court-appointed volunteer advocacy. CASA volunteers are appointed by judges to watch over and work directly with abused and neglected children to provide them a voice and someone consistent to depend upon.

Foster Care Alumni of America

5810 Kingstowne Center Dr., Suite 120-730
Alexandria, VA 22315
phone: (703) 299-6767
website: www.fostercarealumni.org

This group's mission is to connect the foster care alumni community and to work together to transform foster care policy and practices.

National Foster Care Coalition

1220 L St. NW, Suite 100-241
Washington, DC 20005-4018
website: www.nationalfostercare.org

This is a nonpartisan partnership of individuals, organizations, foundations, and associations that are working to improve the lives of the nearly half a million young people currently in the foster care system.

National Youth Advocate Program

1801 Watermark Dr., Suite 200
Columbus, OH 43215
phone: (877) 692-7226
website: www.nyap.org

This organization has provided services to support youth and families since 1978. Specifically, it provides foster care for youth and offers information on how to become a foster parent.

For Further Research

Books

Cris Beam, *To the End of June: The Intimate Life of American Foster Care*. New York: Mariner, 2014.

Regina Calcaterra, *Etched in Sand: A True Story of Five Siblings Who Survived an Unspeakable Childhood on Long Island*. New York: Morrow, 2013.

John DeGarma, *The Foster Parenting Manual*. Philadelphia: Kingsley, 2013.

Kailamai Hansen, *Out of Darkness: My Journey Through Foster Care*. Akron, OH: CreateSpace, 2014.

Kathy Harrison, *Another Place at the Table*. New York: TarcherPerigee, 2004.

Paula McLain, *Growing Up in Other People's Houses*. New York: Back Bay, 2014.

Ashley Rhodes-Courter, *Three Little Words: A Memoir*. New York: Atheneum Books for Young Readers, 2009.

Martha Shirk, *On Their Own: What Happens to Kids When They Age Out of the Foster Care System*. New York: Basic Books, 2006.

Internet Sources

Children's Rights, "Child Abuse and Neglect," 2014. www.childrensrights.org/newsroom/fact-sheets/child-abuse-and-neglect.

Cierra, "A Letter Dedicated to My Guardianship Angel," *Washington Informer*, September 19, 2015. http://washingtoninformer.com/news/2015/sep/16/letter-dedicated-my-guardianship-angel.

Carrie Craft, "Top Reasons Children Enter the Foster Care Program," About Parenting, 2015. http://adoption.about.com/od/fostering/f/why_are_children_in_foster_care.htm.

Jessica Lahey, "Every Time Foster Kids Move, They Lose Months of Academic Progress," *Atlantic*, February 28, 2014. www.theatlantic.com/education/archive/2014/02/every-time-foster-kids-move-they-lose-months-of-academic-progress/284134.

Dave Ranney, "Teens Describe Foster Care Experience," Kansas Health Institute, May 9, 2010. www.khi.org/news/article/teens-share-foster-care-perspective.

Gary Stangler, "Aging Out of Foster Care: The Costs of Doing Nothing Affect Us All," *Huffington Post*, July 28, 2013. www.huffingtonpost.com.

Edward Timpson, "Life as a Foster Family: 'I Became Well-Versed in Most Swear Words,'" *Guardian* (Manchester), March 3, 2015. www.theguardian.com/social-care-network/2015/mar/03/edward-timpson-childrens-minister-foster-family.

Beth Walton, "Finding a Home: Need for Foster Care Outpacing Resources," *Asheville (NC) Citizen-Times*, August 29, 2015. www.citizen-times.com/story/news/local/2015/08/29/finding-home-need-foster-care-outpacing-resources/71383316.

Websites

Foster Care to Success (www.fc2success.org). This website provides information about programs throughout the nation that are in place to help prepare aging-out foster youth for independence.

Foster Youth in Action (www.fosteryouthaction.org). This website gives information on what foster youth are doing to change and improve the foster care system.

Index

Picture Credits

About the Author

Leanne Currie-McGhee lives in Virginia with her husband, Keith; her two daughters, Grace and Hope; and her dog, Delilah. She loves writing educational books for youth and has done so for over a decade.